MAKING LEMONADE FROM EDUCATION'S LEMONS

Ron Nichols

Making Lemonade from Education's Lemons

By

Ron Nichols

Contents

Acknowledgements

First, I want to thank my wife, Aleese, for putting up with me getting multiple degrees and various other education since we have been married.

Secondly, I want to thank everyone who has ever been instrumental in my lifelong learning (teachers, professors, sergeants, pastors, peers).

Lastly, I want to thank God for giving me the desire and ability to learn and comprehend various subjects.

Introduction

Life is a series of learning opportunities. Some of these opportunities are free and others cost. Sometimes those costs can soar into the hundreds of thousands of dollars. Believe me I know.

This book is about my experience in a variety of educational settings. It is my hope that this book will help you narrow your career focus and save you thousands of dollars and countless hours of potentially needless study.

The facts and figures I use in this book came from the internet. You can follow the end note and click on the link to verify the information provided in this book.

Fun Facts: Statistical analysis of education

No high school diploma	$553/week
High school diploma	$730/week
Some college/ no degree	$802/week
Associates degree	$862/week
Bachelor's degree	$1,198/week
Master's degree	$1,434/week
Professional degree	$1,884/week
Doctoral degree	$1,825/week[1]

- These are median earnings. Median means average. Those numbers can fluctuate (go) up or down depending on the area you live in.

   According to Michael B. Sauter, the cost of living in Arkansas is $46,672 per year[2]. That amounts to $897 a week. If you look at the stats above, you will notice that that figure falls in between the associates and bachelor's degree income range. I have to say that his estimate is close. It takes mine and my wife's income to keep everything paid utilities, auto, insurance, mortgage, food, entertainment.

   These numbers are just a rough estimate. The choices you make can cause them to go up or down.

Hillary Hoffower and Allana Akhtar said, "The average student-loan debt per graduating student in 2018 who took out loans is $29,800, according to Student Loan Hero"[3]. They gave an example of how an advanced degree was not worth the trouble of getting when compared to the debt carried by the borrower. According to Hoffower and Akhtar,

> Consider Mike Meru, an orthodontist who owed $1,060,945 in student loans as of May 2018 and is expected to face a $2 million loan balance in the next two decades, The Journal said. Meru's situation shows that, despite high salaries, becoming a doctor, a dentist, or even a lawyer isn't the path to wealth it once was[4].

> His payments over twenty years will be roughly $8,333 per month. Based on our stats from earlier, this financially does not make sense.

Don't know where to start?

You should realize by now that it pays to get an education so that you can provide for yourself and/or family. Maybe you are thinking to yourself that that is all good, but you have no clue where to begin. You can toil away making minimum wage ($9.25/hour in Arkansas) or you can explore your options. What are those options you ask? Glad you asked.

What motivates you? Like to hunt and fish? Game warden. Like fashion? Manage clothing store or design clothes. Work with your hands? Skilled trade (more on that later). Like being in charge? Become a manager. Most fast food places have management programs. Like working by yourself. Become a truck driver.

The possibilities are endless. The main thing is that is choose something that you love doing because life is too short to be stuck in a dead-end job where you max out pay wise and either cannot advance with that company, get let go, or just decide to start all over.

Still stuck? No problem. There are numerous free web sites where you can take a career assessment test to help you determine what you would be best suited for career wise. All it takes is pulling up your favorite search engine, type in career assessment, and take the assessment(s). When I was in high school, the military came to my school and provided a very thorough assessment called the ASVAB (Armed Services Vocational Aptitude Battery). This assessment will yield 3-5 career options for you to choose from. Even if you are not interested in the military, the free test will give you better insight into your future career.

Career aptitude test

What career best fits your personality? This free career aptitude test can give you insight into your career personality. Based on a characterization of your personality in terms of Holland Code personality types, you will learn what kind of work environments and occupations suit you best. The results of this career test provide you with a list of professions and occupations that fit your career personality.

Choose a career that matches your preferences and you will increase your chances of being successful! It takes five to ten minutes to complete.

https://www.123test.com/career-test/

Traditional Education

Traditionally, students are strongly encouraged to go to college after high school by their family, a teacher, or both. According to Wikipedia.org, The definition of *traditional education* varies greatly with geography and by historical period.

> The chief business of traditional education is to transmit to a next generation those skills, facts, and standards of moral and social conduct that adults consider to be necessary for the next generation's material and social success.[2] As beneficiaries of this scheme, which educational progressivist John Dewey described as being "imposed from above and from outside", the students are expected to docilely and obediently receive and believe these fixed answers. Teachers are the instruments by which this knowledge is communicated and these standards of behavior are enforced.[2]5.

The thinking behind this seems logical. We have seen that the more education you have the more money you can make and thus have a better standard of living. Students go to school for twelve years and this is known as primary education. The goal is to earn a diploma and then go to college for four to five years (secondary education).

Traditional students are anywhere from 18 to 25 years old. Traditional education would benefit those who are determined to be doctors or lawyers. It takes seven years of full-time study to become a lawyer and seven or more years to become a doctor (depending on area of specialty).

On campus or online?

There are advantages and disadvantages to going to school on campus or online. Let's look at physically going to school. First, you must drive there (time, gas). Then you have to find a parking spot. (Some campuses charge for parking) You may have to go to an early class. Not a good option if you like sleeping in. This option is good if you are a people person and like structure.

Online has its advantages and disadvantages too. For instance, it requires a lot of discipline, focus to attend online classes. The sweet thing about online classes are that you can attend at your leisure (when it is convenient for you). Every class has assignment deadlines. You will get points subtracted for turning in assignments late. * Most professors will work with you if you tell (email) them about your situation. You will save a lot of time and money attending online classes because you will not have to drive to a physical location to go to classes.

> Online classes are regularly less expensive than traditional classes. Students are spared the high cost of room and board on campus as well as travel expenses. Students are also able to continue working full time while taking online classes, so they may need less financial aid or loans, reducing their debt at graduation[6].

If you are in a hurry to get a degree and a better job this is something to consider.

Online schools often function on a different schedule from traditional schools. Students may be able to spend a month on a class as opposed to 3 months in a traditional setting, plus online classes often allow you to take classes during months that are break times for traditional students, such as January and the summer months. Shorter time from beginning to degree completion means that you'll be on your way to your end goal sooner (and maybe for less money!)[7]

I have attended college on campus and online for many years. When I got my first master's degree, I worked all day and went to class two times a week for thirteen months. I am finishing up my second master's degree online. I personally like the flexibility on going to school online.

You have to experiment and see which you like better.

Community/ 2-year colleges

These colleges are in most major cities and some rural areas. They offer the same level of classes a person can take at a four-year college and cost up to 2/3 less than four-year colleges per semester hour. Most of the time an associate degree from a community college will transfer to a four-year college/university. ** Disclaimer ** You must check with your school to see which hours are transferrable.

Ideally, a student can live at home and go to a two-year college and save a ton of money on living expenses. Also, the lower cost per hour will help too. An associate degree holder makes a little over $300/month than a high school diploma holder.

Some degrees offered at two-year colleges are: Aviation technology, automotive technology, diesel technology, cosmetology, electronics, heat ventilation air conditioning refrigeration, tractor/trailer logistics, and welding. These career fields are crucial to other industries. Trucks need servicing so they can haul goods all across the country. Trains use diesel power and require maintenance.

University/ 4-year colleges

These colleges offer more specific education and the career choices are greater as well. If a student wants to become a doctor or lawyer, they must get an undergraduate (4 year) degree first.

University accreditation is something you need to look into when transferring credits.

Why is accreditation important?
An important factor in realizing a successful career is choosing a reputable college. Colleges that have been through the accreditation process are more likely to offer degrees that employers and recruiters recognize. Companies want to know that you have a quality education and that you will have something to bring to the table when you join their team. For this purpose, accreditation enables companies to filter those individuals who have obtained a degree from an accredited institution from those who have not. The accreditation process also offers students a better chance of having their credits transferred to other reputable institutions should they decide to obtain a graduate or doctoral level education[8].

** In the early 90's, I attended a vocational school and borrowed $10,500. When I went to transfer to a four-year college none of my credits were recognized. I had to start all over.

- Check your school for the proper accreditation!
-

Beyond college: graduate/doctorate

A graduate degree is required if a student wants to go into counseling, business, or some other professional occupation. Counselors with a master's degree cannot prescribe medication to clients.

There are a lot of degree types out there. Many fall into one of two camps: doctorates and master's degrees. Both graduate degrees offer a narrower educational focus than the undergraduate experience. The higher the degree, the longer it takes to earn and the more specialized is its focus. We're taking a closer look at the master's and doctorate degrees to highlight differences and help you determine which might be most useful to you.

Master's degrees are more versatile than doctoral degrees and have a wide range of professional and academic applications. The most common master's degrees are Masters of Arts (M.A.) and Master of Science (M.S.).

The most common doctorate is the Doctor of Philosophy or PhD. These research doctorates prepare students to contribute to the collective knowledge base of the field and offers a unique opportunity for an individual to conduct intensive and prolonged research on a very particular topic, which often leads to publication. Additionally, there are professional doctorates like the MD (Medical Doctor), and the JD (Juris Doctor). Before pursuing a doctorate, candidates must have already earned a bachelor's degree and in some cases a master's depending on the program. Due to the nature of specialization, PhD programs tend to be smaller than master's programs[9].

Alternatives to Traditional Education

Did you know that some trades make as much as doctors? Cheatsheet.com lists five jobs that make more money than doctors and require very little education. First, sales managers/salespeople average $123,150 a year. Managers will need a bachelor's degree. Second, air traffic controllers average $118,650 a year and only require an associate degree. Third, architectural/engineering managers average $136,540 and require a bachelor's degree. Fourth, petroleum engineers average$149,180 a year and require a bachelor's degree. Fifth, CEO's (chief executive officer) average $178,400 and usually have a bachelor's degree[10].

Although doctors earn the highest median annual salaries, they have incredibly high investment and opportunity costs — they give up around half a million dollars to become doctors. We also have to consider the fact that all workers within a specific occupation are not created equally. Some doctors earn more or less than others, and the same goes for workers in other occupations.

NerdWallet discussed a doctor's investment costs in a report a while back, finding that in 2012, 79% of medical school graduates reported education debt of more than $100,000; the average medical school debt was $166,750. If that average debt takes 30 years to pay back, we're talking about at least a $350,000 repayment (at 6% interest, payments of around $1,000 per month, and no missed payments).

Plus, when you add in at least four or five years of missed salaries of around $57,000 per year (the median earnings for someone with a bachelor's degree), this means a doctor gives up at least another $228,000 worth of after-college salaries to complete additional, post-graduate training. Between loans and missed salaries, a doctor's investment costs add up to around $578,000, or around $20,000 per year for 30 years. And this is a conservative estimate[11].

1. Carpenter

Perhaps it's not surprising that carpentry has a bright future. A growing population means additional housing, workplaces, and health care facilities. Innovative technology is changing the types of buildings we live and work in, which means constant renovations and updating. That's on top of the everyday needs we have for carpenters, such as additions to homes and repairs. The future for carpentry is bright.

2. Electrician

Similar to the increased demand in carpenters, industrial and commercial electricians are integral into new and existing construction projects. Electricians also have the unique need to broaden their skillset as technology becomes part of our everyday lives. Think of the ever-changing gadgets we use at home: programmable lights, security systems, remote thermostats. As our lives become more tech savvy—and the line between IT expert and electrician blurs—we'll be relying more and more on these experts.

3. Welder

Welders are essential to construction projects of all types, so their bright future alongside carpenters and electricians makes sense. What you might not realize is that welders can use their skills in a variety of scenarios:

manufacturing cars, production warehouses, building bridges, and other construction sites. Their versatility puts them in high demand and also leaves room for each welder to choose their preferred career path[12].

According to US News, carpenters make an average of $46,590 a year[13]. Acccording to work.chron.com, "As of 2011, electricians earned an average of $52,910 per year, according to the Bureau of Labor Statistics. The average hourly pay for an electrician was estimated to be $25.44"[14]. Welders make serious money. According to gowelding.org,

> Traveling industrial pipe **welders** earn anywhere between $50,000.00 and $185,000.00 a year. Underwater **welders** can earn $100,000.00 to well over $200.000.00 a year. Military support **welders** can start at $160,000.00 to more than $200,000.00 a year in the Middle East[15].

Carpenter training consists of a three to four-year apprenticeship[16]. Electrical training is conducted in the class and on the job over a four-year period[17]. Welding training takes around seven months according to Tulsa Welding School web site[18].

Plumbers make "$50,620 annually"[19]. Plumbers (like electricians) start their careers as apprentices. An apprenticeship lasts roughly four years. Most employers pay for the apprenticeship.

Truck drivers make between $40,000 - $73,000 a year[20]. According to alltrucking.com,

> On average, a Class A CDL program lasts about seven weeks. This is based on full-time programs that run for five days per week. Class A programs tend to last longer than Class B programs, since a Class A license permits you to drive a greater variety of trucks and take on larger loads[21].

Auto mechanics make "between 26,850 to $47,540 a year and require an associate degree[22].

CNA's (certified nurse assistant) make an average of $24,454[23]. According to allnursingschools.com "most certified nursing assistant programs take between four and 12 weeks. This is broken into contact hours and clinic practice"[24]. Registered nurses (RN) require a bachelor's degree and make $71,730 a year[25]. Nurse Practitioner's/Physician's assistants average $104,860 a year and require a master's/doctorate degree[26].

Cosmetologist's average about $14.23 an hour plus tips. Cosmetology training lasts up to two years[27].

Military service pay varies depending on how long you serve, your rank, marital status, career field, and deployment status. The base pay for a private E1 is $20,795 with less than two years of service. A sergeant E5 with over three years makes $33,130 a year. A lieutenant O-1 makes #39,448 with less than two years of service. (These figures are for active duty)[28]. There is extra pay for jumping out of planes, diving, flight, psychologists, combat, medical/dental officers[29].

Active duty affords members opportunities to travel the world for free, make decent money, and get an education. It is possible to get a bachelor's degree while serving on active duty. Usually service members can go to OCS (Officer's Candidate School) or apply for a direct commission as an officer. An O-1 with four years of service makes $49,632 a year compared to a sergeant E5 - $34,695. That is a difference of $14,937 just for letting the military pay you to get an education!

Historically, people worked until age 62 or 65 and retired from working. At that point they would use their social security to live on. The way our government spends money is mind boggling. Personally, I am not counting on social security to be there when I would be eligible to get it.

That may sound a little bleak. What should you do? I would suggest saving a portion of each check in a 401K or some other savings account. A savvy person could join the military part time and stay enlisted for 20-30 years and work a full-time job until they have enough money to retire on. Even though a person retires does not mean they should quit working all together. It is possible to work part-time and/or volunteer after retirement. When I was in college, I learned that people who retire and do not stay active usually die within five years of retiring. You could travel the country, visit family, travel internationally with the money you have put back.

Each branch of the military has its own area of specialization. For instance, the Army and Marines are usually tasked to fight wars and keep peace all over the world. (* Don't get me wrong, The Navy has SEALS, the Air Force has Para Rescue Jumpers, and the Coast Guard has Deployable Specialized Forces[30].) The other branches get deployed too and some of their members see combat. Air Force service members are highly educated, have the best living arrangements, and have short tours overseas. The Navy sails all over the world, has really good food, softens up beaches for the Marines, and provides various forms of support from the sea. The Coast Guard can be mobilized during war but usually stay within the waters surrounding the United States.

Even service members (Guard and Reserve) who enlist part time get deployed overseas to strengthen the active duty members of each branch. If you are hard charging, then the Army or Marines will be a good career choice. If you want to see the world but not fight, the Navy is a good option. If you are super smart and don't like getting dirty, the Air Force is your best bet. If you like the water but don't want to travel the world then join the Coast Guard.

I am kind of fond of the Army because my dad and grandpa were Army paratroopers.

Non-traditional Students

According to the National Center for Education Statistics, <u>non-traditional students are usually 24 and older</u>. As slightly older young adults, many students who attend college at this age have work experience or family situations that can sometimes make attending college full-time difficult. Some of these students may actually hold down full-time jobs and only attend school part-time or on an occasional basis. Unlike younger, more traditional students, they do not often live on campus[31].

Money, Money, Money! Paying for school

A *scholarship* is a type of *financial aid* awarded to students seeking to further their education. They can be awarded on a different basis but most commonly on the basis of academic merit or need for financial aid to cover tuition fees etc. Scholarship money is not repaid to the organization awarding it[32].

A **grant** is a quantity of money, i.e., financial assistance, given by a government, organization, or person for a specific purpose. Unlike a loan, you do not have to pay back the money. In some cases, the receivers of study grants who abandoned their courses have to pay back the money[33].

Work Study

Work-study is a federally and sometimes state-funded program that helps college students with financial need get part-time jobs[34].

If you are still in high school, excellent! The best way to get free money for school is by making good grades and being part of a sport. There are all kinds of scholarships for college for students with good grades (academic) and sports (athletic). There are deadlines to be mindful of when applying for them. The earlier you apply the better.

If you are a non-traditional student, no problem. You will have to fill out the FAFSA (Free Application for Federal Student Aid) through this link https://studentaid.gov/h/apply-for-aid/fafsa You may qualify for a Pell grant. Pell grants are determined based on income.

It is quite possible to get a full ride.

A full-ride scholarship is an award that covers the entire cost of attending college. Cost of attendance (COA) is tuition, room and board, textbooks, fees, meals and other things. For example, some full ride scholarships also pay for a laptop. Funds for personal expenses and stipend for enrichment are common too.

Where can you get a full ride scholarship? There are different sources that award full ride scholarships. The federal government, colleges, and private sources to list a few. As you might expect, they are very competitive, and many students' dream[35].

High school students with high GPA (grade point average) and ACT SAT scores can get a full ride into most colleges.

To be eligible, students must have **ACT scores** of at least 31 or SAT **scores** of at least 1430, be in the top 5% of their high school classes and have a GPA of 3.8 or above. A maximum of six scholarships are given out every year, and the deadline for submission is December 1[36].

Student loan payment options

There are many repayment options when it comes to student loans. There is the traditional method where you pay back a set amount every month for 20-30 years. This option is not advisable because if you borrow $100,000 and pay the $716.43 a month for 20 years you will end up paying an additional $71,943 in interest plus the $100K you borrowed to attend college[37].

Some schools offer to pay off student loans if you agree to teach for a certain number of years. If you can land a job with your state government, the government may pay off your loans after ten years as long as you keep your payments current. If you end up 100% disabled your loans can be discharged.

> If you are totally and permanently disabled, you may qualify for a total and permanent disability (TPD) discharge of your federal student loans or TEACH Grant service obligation. If you receive a TPD discharge, you will no longer be required to repay your loans or complete your TEACH Grant service obligation[38].

- If you have to take out loans, only borrow what you need for school and living expenses. The less you borrow the less you have to pay back.
- Also, you can make extra payments and/or apply your tax returns to your debt to pay it off quicker and save money on interest.

Defaulted loans

Whatever you do, do not default on your student loans. A default is where you quit making payments for a period of time. When you default on student loans:

- **The IRS can withhold tax refunds to pay off the debt.**
- **The Department of Education can garnish your wages very easily.**
- **You might receive lower Social Security payments**
- **Credit score greatly affected[39].**

If you are unable to pay back your loans, contact your lender. Your lender will work with you to postpone or defer your loans payments if you experience a financial setback for whatever reason.

*Be careful not to fall for programs that require you to pay them to get your loans out of default. Many times, contacting your lender will resolve any issues you may have and only takes a phone call.

Career advancement

Let me begin by sharing a true story.

When I was in college, I did not want to do an internship because I had "bills". My pride to work temporarily for free cost me a great deal. In fact, I was talked into getting a master's degree because I was fixing to have to pay back my student loans but did not have the necessary experience to go with my degree. So, I got the master's degree and my pay went up $3/hour. I eventually got better paying jobs, but only after going to trade school.

The moral of my story is this: take an internship for the experience. In fact, some internships are paid. If you do not take an internship it will be hard to get a job. Internships not only give you hands on experience but also help you make connections via networking. When you get to know people, those people know people and most of the time getting that dream job that's going to pay you well is simply a matter of who you know.

It would be hard to explain career advancement for many jobs/careers. I will give you a personal example. When I was in the Army, I learned what I needed to do to advance to the next rank. More rank meant more money and responsibility. I did not have to do anything to advance from private E1 to specialist E4. When I went from specialist to sergeant, I had to do some things. I had to pass my PT (physical fitness test), qualify with my weapon, have medals/awards, have some schooling (college), attend a basic leadership course, and get my commander to write a statement explaining that I was ready for the next higher rank. Each category was worth so many points. I needed a certain number of points to advance to the next higher rank. Once my packet with supporting documentation was submitted, a board reviewed my paperwork and drew up orders stating that I was a sergeant.

(* That was 18 years ago. I am sure things have changed since. Ask your sergeant how he/she got promoted, they will help you.)

Whatever field you end up in there are certain steps you can take to advance your career. Many companies have annual evaluations, quotas, and other requirements for career advancement. If you set yourself apart from your peers, you will advance to the next level. *This does not mean throwing people under the bus and using people to make yourself look good.

It is up to you to find out what your organization looks at as far as advancement.

If you find yourself in a dead-end job, it may be time to look at a different company, change career paths, and/or start your own business.

If I could turn back time

In the last chapter, I cried about having not volunteered my time in exchange for experience. If I were able to go back in time, I would do things a lot differently. Here is what I would do. First, I would have joined the Army part time and let the Army pay for my schooling. Once I got a bachelor's degree, I would use that degree to become an officer in the Army which would involve a three-year active duty commitment. I would ask for a duty assignment in Germany. While in Germany, I would take advantage of the colleges on base and further my education and take the train to France and Spain in my off time. I may even continue learning Spanish so that I could be more marketable as a civilian when I retire or go back to part time military service.

Spiritual dimension and vocation

You are probably asking yourself what I mean by spiritual dimension and vocation. Well, it is simply this, we have been put here on this earth by God. Everything we have or will have is because of Him. He created us for His pleasure. It pleases God when we have a relationship with Him and honor Him with our time, talent(s), and finances.

The Bible says in Jeremiah that God has a plan for us. We can follow our own plan and end up failing in life or we can seek Him for His guidance (His Word promises us that He will guide us if we ask Him to.) Sometimes our calling (a strong inner impulse toward a particular course of action especially when accompanied by conviction of divine influence, the vocation or profession in which one customarily engages[40]) and vocation (job/career) match up and sometimes it doesn't.

If you know you are called to the ministry, chances are you can find full time employment with a church or other Christian organization. If you do not feel a specific calling to ministry, that is ok. Maybe God wants you to work in one of the trades or even a white-collar job and support your local church with your finances.

Maybe you do not know God or His Son Jesus. It may even be possible that you know Him from social media. The truth is that God loves you so much He sent His Son Jesus to die on the cross so you can receive forgiveness of your sins. He wants to have an eternal relationship with you. How do you start a relationship with God/Jesus?

Say this prayer out loud: *"Father, I believe Jesus died on the cross, rose from the dead, and is now seated at your right hand. I ask that you forgive me of all my sins, come into my life, and be my Lord and Savior. Help me to live my life for you. I ask this in the name of Jesus"*.

Congratulations and welcome to the family of God!

I know I have given you a bunch of things to think about as far as school and work. I need to give you a few more things to help you in your new relationship with God.

1) Pray daily. Just talk to God like He is your best friend.
2) Read the Bible. You can download the Bible app to your phone. I like reading from the English Standard Version.
3) Go to church. Find a church near you and learn more about God and develop new friendships with other believers.
4) When you mess up (sin), don't beat yourself up. Simply ask God to forgive you and help you not to keep on sinning.

Father, I ask you to guide my new brothers and sisters in Christ in their calling, bless them with the funds they need to gain an excellent education, and protect them and their families in these last days. I ask this in Jesus' name. Amen

Closing Thoughts

I have a serious problem with diploma mills sucking students in, loading them up with debt, and not able to guarantee them a decent job to help pay off the debt they have racked up. I also have an issue with the traditional approach to education. I also have an issue with all educational systems that fail students and society in general by not educating students in how to make a budget and manage finances including the pitfalls of debt.

Not everyone is cut out for college. As we have seen, there are other options that are equally effective and hundreds of times less expensive than going the traditional route. There is no need to get a degree if you believe you can live on a salary from driving a truck or working in one of the trades. The only exception would be if your company requires it for an upper management position. In that case, work and go to school part time.

If you are still in high school (I hope you are), you can talk to your guidance counselor and start applying for scholarships. The more scholarships you get the better. You could end up getting a "full ride" (not need to borrow money for school)!!! Do not pay for a scholarship service. Do your homework. The school you want to go to offers scholarships, there are books in your library that lists grants and scholarships you can apply for. In Arkansas, some of the lottery money goes to scholarships. Maybe your state offers something like that.

End notes

---

[1] https://www.bls.gov/emp/tables/unemployment-earnings-education.htm

[2] https://www.usatoday.com/story/money/economy/2018/05/10/cost-of-living-value-of-dollar-in-every-state/34567549/

[3] https://www.businessinsider.com/student-loan-debt-crisis-college-cost-mind-blowing-facts-2019-7

[4] https://www.businessinsider.com/student-loan-debt-crisis-college-cost-mind-blowing-facts-2019-7

[5] https://en.wikipedia.org/wiki/Traditional_education

[6] https://www.collegeraptor.com/getting-in/articles/online-colleges/is-online-college-right-for-you-pros-and-cons-of-going-to-college-online/

[7] Ibid.

[8] https://www.50states.com/college-resources/accreditation.htm

[9] https://www.idealist.org/grad-schools/blog/difference-masters-doctorate

[10] https://www.cheatsheet.com/money-career/jobs-that-make-more-money-than-doctors.html/

[11] Ibid.

[12] https://www.peopleready.com/blogs/associate-blog/3-in-demand-jobs-in-skilled-trades

[13] https://money.usnews.com/careers/best-jobs/carpenter/salary

[14] https://work.chron.com/much-electricians-earn-annually-7534.html

[15] https://www.google.com/search?q=welders+salary&rlz=1C1PRF I_enUS837US838&oq=welders+salary&aqs=chrome..69i57j0l7.6 049j0j4&sourceid=chrome&ie=UTF-8

[16] https://studentscholarships.org/careers_salary/195/education/ carpenters.php

[17] https://www.electriciancareersguide.com/how-long-does-it-take-to-become-an-electrician/

[18] https://www.weldingschool.com/programs/professional-welding-training/

[19] https://www.ferguson.com/content/trade-talk/business-tips/how-much-money-do-plumbers-make

[20] https://money.cnn.com/2015/10/09/news/economy/truck-driver-shortage/index.html

[21] http://www.alltrucking.com/faq/how-long-to-get-cdl/

[22] https://work.chron.com/education-requirements-auto-mechanics-14930.html

[23] https://www.monster.com/career-advice/article/certified-nurse-assistant-salary

[24] https://www.allnursingschools.com/certified-nursing-assistant/degrees/

[25] https://money.usnews.com/careers/best-jobs/registered-nurse/salary

[26] https://www.allnursingschools.com/nurse-practitioner/salary/

[27] https://work.chron.com/much-cosmetologist-make-per-year-8049.html

[28] https://www.militaryrates.com/military-pay-charts-o1_o5_2020

[29] https://myarmybenefits.us.army.mil/Benefit-Library/Federal-Benefits/Special-Pay?serv=122

[30] https://www.military.com/special-operations/deployable-operations-group.html

[31] https://www.bestvalueschools.com/faq/what-does-it-mean-to-be-a-non-traditional-student/

[32] https://scholarshipfellow.com/scholarship-definition/

[33] https://marketbusinessnews.com/financial-glossary/grant-definition-meaning/

[34] https://www.nerdwallet.com/blog/loans/student-loans/what-is-work-study/

[35] https://www.unigo.com/scholarships/by-type/full-ride-scholarships

[36] blog.prepscholar.com › colleges-with-full-ride-scholarships

[37] https://www.bankrate.com/calculators/college-planning/loan-calculator.aspx

[38] https://www.disabilitydischarge.com/

[39] https://www.thebalance.com/what-happens-when-you-default-on-a-loan-315393

[40] https://www.merriam-webster.com/dictionary/calling

Other books by Ron Nichols

Making Lemonade from Life's Lemons

Making Lemonade from your Lemons: A 45 Day Devotional

About the Author

R. K. Nichols is a follower of Christ. He is an avid tither and firmly believes in Malachi 3: 8-10. He is a husband, dad, and grandpa. He is a hardworking man. He is a driven man. He is an educated man. He is also a traveled man, having been to five countries.

He has had some lessons throughout his educational journey. He has not let those lemons deter him in his walk with the Lord. He spent many years and borrowed thousands of dollars on his education he is finally in a place where it will pay off.

He is a man with a higher purpose and knows what he is called to do. He is passionate about winning the lost to Christ, as evidenced by his door-to-door witnessing, missions trip to the Philippines, and regular financial contributions to various Christian organizations that are committed to spreading the Word of God all over the world, especially the 1040 window.

One of his favorite scriptures is Matthew 6:33, "Seek ye first the kingdom of God and all these things shall be added unto you." He currently is finishing his second master's degree (M. DIV.), a businessman, an ordained minister, and a future house church pastor.

(Back cover – remove)

In *Making Lemonade from Education's Lemons,* the author chronicles his educational experience following high school. The author explains many of the setbacks he had throughout his educational journey,

The author has been in school in one form or another for over 27 years. His education consisted of military, college, and vocational learning.

Looking back, the author wished he would have done things differently concerning his education. He said he would have gone part time In the Army Reserves and let the military pay for his schooling and use it to further his military career. He also would have gone to trade school in his twenties instead of his forties.

The author hopes that his brief book will save his readers many years (time) and many dollars (money) in their pursuit of getting an education and providing for their families.

www.ingramcontent.com/pod-product-compliance
Lightning Source LLC
Chambersburg PA
CBHW060634030426
42337CB00018B/3362